THE WOMAN
&
HER PASTOR

10 Blocks for Building a Positive Relationship with
Your Male Pastor

MARCIA ESTRADA

The Woman & Her Pastor
10 Blocks for Building a Positive Relationship with Your Male Pastor
ISBN-13: 978-1503340077
ISBN-10: 1503340074
Copyright © 2011 by Marcia Estrada

Published by
Ashley Estrada Ministries
PO Box 582086
Kissimmee, FL 34758
www.ashleyestradaministries.com

DEDICATION

This book is lovingly dedicated to my husband and best friend of over thirty-five years, Apostle Ashley C. Estrada who has given me every opportunity to fulfill the call of God upon my life. From him I have learned much of what is said in this book. It is also dedicated to the memory of my mother, Mary Samuel Cambridge who went to be with the Lord on December 14, 2000. She showed me by example what it means to be a good wife. I dedicate it to my children, Joel, Kenneth, Kristel, Jesse and Jeriah who have experienced what it is to be "pastors' kids." I also dedicate this book to the people of Kingdom Life International Christian Center, Inc., St. Thomas, United States Virgin Islands and Kissimmee, Florida, who have grown and are continuing to grow together with us in the principles of the Kingdom of God.

CONTENTS

ACKNOWLEDGMENTS

First of all I want to thank the Lord Jesus Christ who has been my Savior since I was eight years old and who counted me faithful in that He has allowed me to serve him in ministry alongside my husband, Apostle Ashley C Estrada for more than thirty-five years and who has never given up on me even when I allowed years to pass before I finally completed this book.

I want to thank my husband who has always encouraged me to share the gift that is in me and has always validated me everywhere he goes to minister the Word.

I want to thank my son, Pastor Kenneth Estrada of Kingdom Life International Center, Poinciana, Florida who did all of the design and layout of this book and who saw to it that it was published and my daughter, Lynette, his wife, thanks for your belief in me.

I also wish to acknowledge Laurel Dorsett of St. Kitts, West Indies who was the very first person who said to me, "You should write a book on this subject", Pastor Gladstone Hazel of Christian Fellowship Church, St. Thomas, who was the next person to encourage me to write this book. Apostle Vonnie James, Minister Angela Rawlings and Evangelist Joan Peters, all of whom helped to birth in me the belief that I can do it.

Finally to the Kingdom Life family in St. Thomas and Florida, you are examples of how to relate positively to your pastors. I love you all.

FOREWORD

I was one of the scheduled speakers at a Women's Conference in St. Thomas and had already delivered my message, when the organizer of the Conference called me and asked me whether I would fill in for another speaker who was unable to make it. She told me the topic was "How to Relate to Your Male Pastor". I agreed to fill in for the speaker and sat down that night with my heart and mind open to the Lord. That is when the Lord inspired me to write down Ten Building Blocks to building a good relationship with your male pastor. The response to the message was phenomenal. I knew it was not me but the Lord, because much of what I said, I had not even written in my notes.

Since that first message, I have shared this message in various forms at other churches, at a Ministers' Conference in New York and at our home church. However, I could never get away from the voices of those who urged me to put it in writing.

I have written this book in fits and starts_ a couple of chapters here, then nothing for months. I have written chapters on planes, at home and in my office. Yet the message has been burned so deeply in my heart that I have never lost the sense of passion that I had that first day when I preached it to that group of women in St. Thomas.

When I sat down to write the last two chapters, determined that I was going to complete this book, I discovered that I had lost the original from the hard drive of my computer. But I was determined not to allow the enemy to have any victory. I believe that the Lord wants this book in the hands of sincere women of God in every church. I know that both men and women can benefit from reading it. I trust that it will be a blessing to you as it has blessed the lives of those who have heard me minister these truths.

CHAPTER 1

THE WOMAN AND HER RELATIONSHIP WITH MEN

Godly women have always played and will always play a vital role in the lives of men and women of God. Apostles, prophets, evangelists, pastors and teachers are Christ's gift to His Church and it is important that we understand the purpose of the gifts and learn how to relate positively to those gifts.

Women, by reason of their great involvement in the activities of the church, must interact and relate to these men of God, in particular, to pastors. However, it is important that we relate in a way that is positive and glorifying to God, the Father.

The relationship you have with your pastor, in many areas is not unlike the relationship you should have with your father or husband. That is why, if you have a negative attitude to men, especially to the authoritative male figures who are or have been in your life, you will have difficulty relating with your male pastor.

Therefore, the first thing I want you to do is to honestly examine the kinds of relationships which you have had with men. Were they positive and healthy ones? What is your pattern of behavior when dealing with men?

THE CLINGER

Are you a clinger? My definition of a clinger is the kind of woman who gives a man the impression that she is so totally helpless without him. She depends on him for almost every detail of her life. She becomes offended if he does not give her an inordinate amount of attention. She uses tears to gain his sympathy and attention. She feels

insecure if he is away from her for any extended period of time.

THE CLIMBER

Are you a climber? I define this kind of woman as the type that

uses a man for her personal benefit. She sees him as a means to

achieving promotion, whether it is in the area of social status,

economic standing, spiritual recognition or employment opportunities.

Her feelings for the man are tied up in what he can add to her and not

what she can add to him.

THE CHANGER

Are you a changer? Some women see a man as a challenge.

They constantly foster relationships with men who have serious flaws

in their lives. He may be an alcoholic or a drug user. He may have the

reputation of being a philanderer or an abuser. The more obvious the

fault, the more excited she becomes at the prospect of being the one

woman who is able to change him. And so, despite all admonitions,

13

The Woman and Her Pastor

she encourages and goes into a relationship with this man with the sole intention of changing him, only to end up frustrated and disillusioned when she realizes that she cannot succeed.

THE CHEATER

Are you a cheater? Is it difficult for you to remain faithful to one man? The cheater starts a relationship with a man fully convinced that this time she has found "Mr. Right" but soon she begins to compare him with other men past and present. She finds him to be boring, not as attractive or considerate or romantic as other men towards whom she finds herself gravitating. It is only a matter of time before she finds that she is cheating on him.

THE CONTROLLER

Are you a controller? The controlling woman can appear to be very soft-spoken and even gentle in her ways or she may appear to be very aggressive. Her outward appearance is not what matters. It is the end result of her interaction with the men in her life. She is driven by the need to control. She may use different methods such as tears, quarrelling, withdrawal, withholding of sexual favors, demeaning remarks or flattering words, but the intent is to get the man to bow to her will in a matter. Until she achieves that she makes his life miserable.

THE CO-WORKER

Are you a co-worker? God's purpose in creating the woman for the man was to make him "a helpmeet for him" a suitable help, someone who would come alongside to help him. The key word is "help" not control or change. I heard this remark years ago and although I do not know the source, I have always remembered it. "God did not take the woman out of the man's head for her to rule over him, nor from his feet for him to make her a door mat, but from his side so that she would be equal to him and be a help suitable for him." A co-worker can relate to a man on the level of equality, without becoming disrespectful, pushy or bossy. She knows how to offer suggestions and gracefully yield if her suggestions are not accepted. She understands that the end result is to get the job done, effectively, efficiently and

excellently and is not intimidated by her partner's skills, abilities and

qualities. She is confident in knowing that she has much to offer to the

relationship and that much will be accomplished if she is given the

opportunity to work together with the man in her life.

WHAT'S NEXT?

After you have honestly examined these descriptions, ask

yourself the question, "Into which category do I fall?" Because you are

a saved, spirit-filled woman of God does not necessarily mean that you

have overcome negative patterns of behavior in your life. Anointing

does not affect character. Character change is the result of the Holy

Spirit being allowed to produce His fruit, and not just His gifts in our

lives. If those patterns of behavior still exist, you will find yourself

transferring them into your relationship with your pastor.

You may try to cling to him and be very offended when he does

not give you all the attention which you want from him. If you are a

climber you may cultivate a relationship with your pastor only because you see it as a means to a position in the church. You may join a church but set out to change the pastor. If you are a cheater you will move from church to church never remaining faithful to any one pastor. You may try to control your pastor if this is your mode of operation. If these patterns of behavior still exist, you will find yourself transferring them into your relationship with your pastor and just as they have created problems with other male figures in your life, they will create problems in your relationship with your pastor. But if you are a co-worker, you will know how to contribute your time, talents and substance to the ministry knowing that you are a "laborer together with him".

I am going to share ten building blocks that are necessary in building a positive relationship with your male pastor. However this book can just as easily read as "How to Build a Positive Relationship with your Husband or with your Father". But before I introduce those building blocks to you, I need to tell you about the foundation upon which those blocks must be laid if the structure is going to be a strong and enduring one.

The Woman and Her Pastor

CHAPTER 2

FORGIVENESS.....
A NECESSARY FOUNDATION

Anyone who knows anything about construction knows that a building is only as good as its foundation. As it is in the natural so it is in the spiritual. A woman will have difficulty relating to her male pastor if she is carrying un-forgiveness, bitterness, or resentment in her heart towards men who have hurt or harmed her in some way. Many more women than those who tell their stories, have been in abusive relationships with men. Many have been hurt or betrayed by men whom they have admired and respected. Some have been sexually molested in their childhood by their fathers, brothers, uncles, ministers, teachers, policemen, doctors, or some male authority figure in their lives. Many more have been or still are in marriages where their husbands verbally or physically or psychologically abuse them.

Many women come to the Lord after they have been through torturous divorce settlements in which husbands strip them of all their happy memories. Some women have been left at altars, left with babies and small children, left with bills, left for another woman and more frequently today, left for another man. Is it any wonder that some women view all men as suspects? They struggle with ambivalent feelings. They are unable to suppress the natural attraction, yet they are apprehensive and distrust any man who offers his friendship or love.

Male pastors are in a caring profession. They often offer gestures of sympathy, caring and understanding. Pastors often allow themselves a measure of demonstrative affection such as a pat on the shoulder, a warm handshake and in some instances, even a hug.

Women who have been traumatized in their relationships with men, can have strong responses to such actions. They can be deluded into thinking that the pastor is romantically interested in them. Or they can respond negatively to the pastor because they associated his words, or gestures with a former relationship that was painful to them.

IT BEGINS WITH A DECISION

Christian women must make a decision to forgive the men who have hurt or betrayed them in some way. Until we do, we cannot be fully effective in our service to the Lord. Women who are holding feelings of resentment against men, will find it very challenging to give truly spiritual counsel to other women who are experiencing difficulties in their marriages. There is a very real danger in which their counsel can be clouded by their own painful memories.

I have listened to wonderful women of God who attempt to defend their ministry of the Word as if anticipating that the men in the congregation will reject them. I have listened with a grieved spirit as some female preachers have upbraided, downgraded and denigrated

21

men in their sermons, all because they ministered from a bruised and

broken spirit.

BEFORE YOU DECIDE TO SERVE YOUR PASTOR

Before you decide to serve your pastor in any capacity, be

healed! Forgive! No woman can claim to be in the Kingdom of God if

she is not forgiven. No woman can fully realize her potential in God if

she refuses to forgive others. Forgiveness is the foundation upon

which the Kingdom of God is built.

1 Tim 1:15
15 Here is a trustworthy saying that deserves full acceptance:
Christ Jesus came into the world to save sinners-of whom I am the
worst.
NIV

NOT A FEELING

Let me share a secret with you that may release you.

Forgiveness is not a feeling it is a choice. It is an act of our will and does

not necessarily involve our emotions. We decide to forgive someone,

to release them and no longer hold them accountable for what they did. We drop the judgment or the charges which we had against them and decide not to seek or wish vengeance upon them.

This does not mean that you will feel for them what you feel for your friends. It does not even mean that you must fellowship with the individual. All of us make choices concerning the people we cultivate as friends.

We choose to fellowship with individuals on various levels. We can fellowship with sinners with the aim of drawing them to the Lord. However we will not involve ourselves in the things that they do or in the ungodly conversations that they hold. We fellowship with some believers more than with others, because there are certain "unbelieving" believers who engage in gossip, complaining, fault-finding and who will dry us up spiritually if we spend too much time in their presence.

Therefore we are not guilty if we know that we have forgiven someone, but wisdom dictates to us that we should not resume fellowship with that individual on the same level that we will fellowship with someone who has our welfare at heart. Ladies, this means that you do not have to remarry your ex-husband whom you have forgiven!

Forgiveness is the foundation that is necessary for us to enjoy a level of freedom and release in our Christian lives. It is the key to effective ministry to others. Christianity is people-based. Churches are made up of people. People will offend each other. Jesus warned us that offenses will come.

Matt 18:7
7 Woe to the world because of offenses! For offenses must come, but woe to that man by whom the offense comes!
NKJV

Woe means sorrow. When we offend we bring sorrow to the one we offend and also to ourselves. That is why Jesus taught us that if we have been offended by someone, we should go to that individual and tell him his fault privately. If he does not hear us, we should take along a witness. If he still does not want to be reconciled we should take him before the church or the spiritual authority. If he still refuses to listen, we are then free. (Matthew 18: 15 – 17)

We are also instructed concerning the course of action we should take when we become aware of the fact that we have offended someone. We are told to leave our gift (money, talent, or ministry) at the altar and be reconciled to our brother and then return to offer our gifts.

Matt 5:22-25
23 Therefore if you bring your gift to the altar, and there remember that your brother has something against you,
24 leave your gift there before the altar, and go your way. First be reconciled to your brother, and then come and offer your gift.
NKJV

HIGH PREMIUM

Our Heavenly Father puts such a high premium on our relationship with each other, especially in the area of forgiveness that He links His willingness to forgive us with our willingness to forgive others.

Matt 6:14
Your heavenly Father will forgive you if you forgive those who sin against you; but if you refuse to forgive them, he will not forgive you.
TLB

Look down through the tunnel of your past. Is there any one that you have not forgiven? It may be that you have forgiven him but you are still holding a judgment against him. You continue to talk about what he did to you. Can his face, voice, or memory cause your heart to skip a beat? Does it cause your palms to sweat, your breath to quicken _ not because of pleasant memories, but past experiences that continue to haunt you? If so, you may still be harboring un-forgiveness in your heart. Once and for all confess it out loud and proclaim your forgiveness of that individual including the fact that you are dropping all charges which you had against him.

The Woman and Her Pastor

The Woman and Her Pastor

CHAPTER 3

BUILDING BLOCK #1
PRAY FOR YOUR PASTOR

The best way I know to build a positive relationship with anyone

is to pray for that person. I learned this lesson while still in my teens.

There was a young man at my home church who annoyed me most of

the time. I repeatedly voiced my resentment towards him by saying, "I

can't stand him". One day my older sister remarked to me, "Why don't

you pray for him?" Because of my admiration for her, I decided to do

as she had suggested. To my surprise, I started to feel differently about

the young man. Though I rarely ever see him, to this day, I consider

him to be one of my good friends.

<u>YOUR MOST IMPORTANT MINISTRY</u>

The most important thing you can do for your pastor is to pray for him. The most important ministry you can have in the church is to pray for your pastor. Pastors need prayer. In fact pastors need much prayer. Pastors go through tests that they are afraid to share with another pastor. Unfortunately, in some cases, they are unable to share with their wives, since she may be the subject or object of their problem. My sister used to tell me, "flesh is flesh and saved flesh is still flesh". I didn't understand what she meant until I grew older. I now know that we have to understand that men of God are prone to discouragement, anxiety, fear, sin, and all the challenges that assail the very people that they are called to minister to. What makes it even more difficult for pastors is that often they have no one with whom they can honestly bare their hearts. Many have no friend with whom they can share the fears and temptations that they go through. Many pastors have discovered, to their sorrow, that it is dangerous to consider members of their congregations as friends. What is even sadder, is that there are few pastors who can confide their secret weaknesses to another minister.

BEHIND THE SCENES

I want you to see a man who is constantly bombarded with problems and needs of his flock's marital and family problems, financial problems, legal problems, and health problems. He is expected to be counselor, accountant, lawyer and doctor. Additionally he may have to deal with an unsympathetic board of directors, an inept or untrustworthy assistant, a complaining wife, seemingly uncontrollable children and yet must come to the pulpit two or three times a week with "a word from the Lord". He may have to conduct prayer meeting when his body is tired or sick. He may be called upon to pray for people when he feels as though God is not hearing him. He must encourage the people to give offerings even when the weight of his own financial needs are great or when he is accused of mismanaging or misusing church funds. He must smile and shake hands even when the weight of his problems seems greater than he can bear.

YOUR MISSION... SHOULD YOU ACCEPT IT

Such a man needs prayer. Prayer for your pastor must not be an afterthought tacked on to your regular prayer. It must take the form of supplication, intercession and strong groaning. Prayer for your pastor should be offered up with the understanding that if "the shepherd is struck the sheep will be scattered" (Matt. 26:31).

The best thing you can do for your pastor is to pray for him, fervently, incessantly and with understanding. It is difficult to hate a man whom you sincerely pray for on a daily basis. Pray for his relationship with his wife because severe attacks come against him in that area. Pray for his children because they are the objects of scrutiny. Pray for his prosperity because a poor pastor, contrary to common opinion, will have difficulty influencing his community and remaining free from the influence of powerful men and women who control his finances. Pray for his good health. Pray for God to grant him favor and good understanding with everyone. Pray for God to open effectual doors for him. Pray for sensitivity to the Spirit of God and the voice of God. Pray against the spirit of discouragement and intimidation, the fear of man, the attacks of the devil, temptation, the spirit of accident and sudden death. You cannot run out of things to pray for, if you really commit yourself to uphold the man of God with your prayers.

A CHANGE OF PERSPECTIVE

As you begin to pray for your pastor, you will begin to see him through different eyes. You will begin to receive his teaching with greater joy. You will be able to accept his correction with more humility. You will be able to view his failings with more grace. You will find it difficult to gossip about him.

If your pastor says something you do not agree with or makes a decision that seems unwise to you, your response should be to pray for him not to upbraid him. In praying for your pastor, you must be careful that your prayer is not tinged with a desire to control him, or to bend him to do your will. You must also understand that it is not your responsibility to try to change him, for that is the work of the Holy Spirit.

CONTINUE EARNESTLY

The apostle Paul whom we consider to be such a mighty man of God asked the Thessalonians to pray for him (1 Thess. 5:25) He admonished the Colossians to "continue earnestly in prayer, being vigilant in it with thanksgiving; meanwhile praying for us that God would open to us a door for the word, to speak the mystery of Christ, for which I am also in chains, that I may make it manifest as I ought to speak" (Col. 4: 3 – 4). We can almost hear the earnest petition of his heart as he covets the prayer of those he has ministered to so many times.

Will you hear the cry of your pastor? Will you commit yourself to pray earnestly for him? Do you want to build a positive relationship with your male pastor? Pray for him.

He needs prayer more than he needs another Sunday School teacher, or Women's Ministries president. For when you pray for Him, you touch the heart of God, and when you touch the heart of God, all things are possible.

The Woman and Her Pastor

The Woman and Her Pastor

CHAPTER 4

BUILDING BLOCK #2
LOVE YOUR
PASTOR.......'S WIFE

I have been a pastor's wife for more than thirty - five years and I have a confession to make. I have a deep, dark secret that I'm going to share with you, my readers and it is this. I have a problem with women in the church and men too, who claim that they love their pastor so much but refuse to show love to the pastor's wife.

Church members have all kinds of reasons for disliking the

pastor's wife. She does not sing and play the piano. She thinks she sings and plays the piano too well. She dresses too ostentatiously. She dresses too dowdily. She is not involved in church matters. She is too involved in the affairs of the church. She lets any and everybody take care of her children. She does not allow anybody to come close to her children. She cannot take care of her home. She has too many helpers to do her household chores. She is unfriendly. She is too friendly with the members, she must be gossiping with them. The list can go on and on, and for every positive characteristic that she has, someone can find reason to see a fault in it.

A WALK IN HER "HIGH-HEELED SHOES"

A pastor's wife is probably one of the most maligned, misunderstood and abused women on the planet. She is constantly in the public eye and she comes into a situation in which she is expected to fulfill the expectations of so many people. In most cases she has had no formal training for her executive position but must fill the role of wife of the chief executive officer. She must be a "good" mother while filling in as counselor, organizer of social events, entertainer of frequent household guests, Sunday School teacher, choir director, and women's president. She may be in the uncomfortable position of having a special anointing or gift in her life which she is not free to express either because of the policies of her church or her husband's personal opinion. She may be in the more favorable position where she is free to function in her calling but must have a lot of wisdom to avoid any signs of competitiveness, control, or overstepping lines of authority.

The pastor's wife must not be a jealous woman. She cannot be jealous of her husband's time or of his associations, whether they are with male or female members of the church. Yet she must know how to communicate her needs to her husband in the spirit of love.

SHE LIVES WITH THE MAN

Love your pastor's wife. She is the person who lives with your pastor every day. She is the one who must encourage him when he is down, bear the brunt of his mood swings, provide comfort for him, satisfy his sexual desires and be a listening ear for whatever troubles he is experiencing. She may perceive that her husband is being taken advantage of, and yet must demonstrate forgiveness to those who have hurt him. She has to guard her children from the disappointing behaviors of church folks so that they will not become bitter and resentful towards the church.

Love your pastor's wife. There are many times when someone may be in grave danger or at the point of death and their family, at any hour, most naturally turns to the pastor to help them through traumatic events. But your pastor's wife has also had her sleep interrupted many times by persons who call at all hours of the night for trivial things. It is a standing joke in our household that one night a young lady called our home after midnight. When my husband picked up the phone anticipating that it was an emergency, the young lady on the other line simply wanted to know where she could she find a certain scripture reference.

Some pastors never turn off their phones off. Today, it's not just the home phone that is a source of distraction but cell phones and other digital devices. Consequently, a pastor's wife can be distracted during her time of passion and miss out on her sexual gratification due to the thoughtlessness of people who do not understand that the pastor and his wife have a life too.

Love your pastor's wife. She may not be pretty, or talented. She may not be as gifted as another pastor's wife. I have had members of another church approach me and try to compare their pastor's wife unfavorably with me. And I've always had to correct them and to let them know that all pastor's wives are not called to preach or to teach.

SHOW HER SOME LOVE

Your pastor's wife may not even seem very loveable but show love to her anyway. Find out her love language. If it is gifts, bring her thoughtful gifts. If it is acts of service, help her. If it is words of affirmation, compliment her. If it is physical touch, give her a hug or kiss after church. If it is quality time or conversation, invite her out to lunch with you one day or invite her to go shopping with you. Try to break through any walls she may have built around her heart because of past hurts and rejection. Her happiness is important to the success of her husband and the ministry he has in his care. An unhappy, disagreeable wife can ruin the best pastor and make him miss out on God's will. Pastors' wives have influenced their husbands to resign from churches contrary to the will of the Lord. Many ministers' marriages are ending up in the divorce courts of the land because of "irreconcilable differences" and even adultery.

If you want to build a positive relationship with your male pastor, you can help by first of all deciding to love your pastor's wife. Love is not a feeling. Love is 1 Corinthians 13. You can choose to love your pastor's wife for the Kingdom's sake.

I HAD MY OWN ISSUES

In the first few years of ministry I struggled with my own issues.

It took me a while to realize that I was coming across to some people in the congregation as being an unfriendly person. I was shocked! I felt I was being misjudged. But I eventually had to face the truth. I realized that I had to change my behavior.

I tend to be very single minded and have difficulty multi-tasking. As I became busier in my role as an administrator, there was always some task before or after services that I had to focus on. Consequently, while my husband, who is a very out-going person, would remain and chat with the folks, I was usually headed to the office to take care of a matter. I did not realize it at the time, but I would go past individuals without stopping to say hello, and without making eye contact because I was so intent on getting to my task. I remember going grocery shopping with my husband and meeting up with acquaintances. My husband would stop and chat but I would become agitated after a while and make my excuses and go on with my shopping until he said his goodbyes and caught up with me again.

Of course I thought he was being very unfair when he

confronted me about my actions and suggested that it was my behavior which was contributing to the reputation I was gaining as being unfriendly. "If they would only get to know me they would know I was not unfriendly", I thought. And yes some people did. Some people were able to look past my behavior. They did not know it but I struggled with one-on-one relationships. While most people would faint if they had to speak to a large audience, I had loved the stage since I was a child. But I was petrified of striking up a conversation with one person.

I'm so grateful to those individuals who loved me in spite of my weakness in that area. And yes, I did go on to make great strides in that area. I coached myself to focus on people, to postpone tasks and to just step outside of my comfort zone. I'm still not there yet. I don't think I'll ever be the kind of person my husband is. But I've come a long way.

So I'll end by saying love your pastor's wife. She has her unique personality but if you make an effort to get to know her, I'm sure you

The Woman and Her Pastor

will find her easy to love.

The Woman and Her Pastor

CHAPTER 5

BUILDING BLOCK #3
RESPECT YOUR PASTOR

The apostle Paul had a problem with the Corinthian church.

They were a gifted church but they did not respect him.   Read what

Paul wrote in 2 Cor. 10: 1-2.

> *2 Cor. 10:1-2*
> *1 I plead with you-yes, I, Paul-and I plead gently, as Christ himself*
> *would do. Yet some of you are saying, "Paul's letters are bold*
> *enough when he is far away, but when he gets here he will be afraid*
> *to raise his voice!"*
> *2 I hope I won't need to show you when I come how harsh and*

rough I can be. I don't want to carry out my present plans against some of you who seem to think my deeds and words are merely those of an ordinary man.
TLB

WE'VE LOCATED THE PROBLEM

The problem with the Corinthian church was that they saw Paul only from the perspective of the flesh. The problem with our churches today is that many people see their pastors from the perspective of the flesh. They do not understand that he walks in an office and that there is an authority that comes with the office.

Familiarity is the chief cause of disrespect. Jesus experienced this when he went to his home town. They failed to see Him in His true office of Messiah. They only saw Him as Joseph's and Mary's son and as the brother of James and the others. Their limited perception of Him limited their ability to receive from Him, for the Scripture records in Mark 6:5 that He could do no mighty miracles there, except that He put His hand on a few sickly folk (suffering from minor illnesses) and healed them. His home town missed the opportunity to give Him a hero's welcome because they did not respect the anointing upon His life.

This scenario is played out again and again in churches around the world. Some members view the pastor as a hired hand. They hired him and they can fire him at will. Since those that preach the gospel must live by the gospel, pastors who are in such a position often find their effectiveness minimized because they may be tempted to compromise their stand because of the insecurity of their position.

"I'M FRIENDS WITH MY PASTOR"

Even if your pastor allows you into the circle of his friends, you must be very careful to draw the line between friendship and familiarity. Do not flaunt your friendship with the pastor by showing off in front of the other members. Do not call him by his first name or some other nickname before those who do not have such a relationship with him. Do not put him in a position where you expect him to sacrifice his integrity upon the altar of your friendship.

<u>OUT OF ORDER</u>

There are some people who flagrantly show disrespect to the pastor. They constantly oppose whatever he tries to initiate in the church. They backbite him to other members and even to unbelievers. They disobey his directives. They disobey and disregard those he has appointed in positions of leadership. Yet they continue to fellowship with the church. This is totally inexcusable.

If a young woman cannot respect her father, she should not remain in his house, accepting food, shelter and clothing from him. Likewise, if you belong to a local house of worship and you have no respect for the man of God who has the oversight of the house, you should not remain there.

You are out of order and more seriously, you are setting yourself up for a painful correction from the Lord. God has reserved certain rights for Himself even as He reserved the Tree of the Knowledge of Good and Evil in the Garden of Eden for Himself. God knows that the men whom He has set over His work will fail Him at times. They may even sin against Him. Yet He has given a command that we should not touch His anointed nor do His prophets harm. (Psa. 105:5)

Paul instructed Timothy in 1 Timothy 5:1 "Rebuke not an elder, but exhort him as a father" (ASV).

WHOSE SERVANT IS HE?

Obviously there is a level of respect with which pastors and other men of God should be treated. Even if your pastor is wrong in a decision which he takes, it is not your business to take him to task. He is not **your** servant.

> *Rom 14:4*
> *4 Who are you to judge someone else's servant? To his own master he stands or falls. And he will stand, for the Lord is able to make him stand.*
> *NIV*

> *Rom 14:4*
> *4 They are God's servants, not yours. They are responsible to him, not to you. Let Him tell them whether they are right or wrong. And God is able to make them do as they should.*
> *TLB*

Which one of us will stand by and allow someone else to upbraid our employees or give them instructions concerning the work which we have assigned them to do? We will be very upset. We will think that such a person is totally out of order and lacking in propriety. Yet we feel that we have the right to chastise God's servants, to treat them as though they are lackeys and to malign and vilify them with or without provocation.

God takes this personally. It is no wonder that persons who habitually set themselves up in churches to be a thorn in the flesh of the pastor, never grow spiritually. Many times their sins affect their children and cause sickness and premature death in their lives. "For this cause many are weak and sickly among you and some have even died, not discerning the Lord's body." (1 Cor. 11:30)

What is the Lord's Body? Religious tradition makes us believe that this refers to the body of Jesus that was nailed to the cross. Others think that this verse of Scripture refers to the wafer or bread that we eat at the Lord's Supper. But the Lord's Body is His Church. It is made up of believers and of the five-fold ministry, apostles, prophets, evangelists, pastors and teachers whom He gave as gifts to the Church. God has a sign over His servants _ HANDLE WITH CARE!

If you are serious about building a positive relationship with your pastor, you must respect your pastor.

MOSES AND MIRIAM

Since this book is addressed primarily to women I thought I would remind my female readers of the story of Miriam and Moses. Miriam was the sister of Moses. She was instrumental in saving his life when their mother had placed him in a basket rather than kill him as Pharoah had ordered. She was instrumental in arranging for their mother to take care of Moses for Pharoah's daughter who found the child and adopted him.

However, when God elevated Moses to the level of emancipator and the leader of his people, Miriam did not make the shift from seeing Moses as her little brother, to seeing him as God's appointed and anointed leader. She therefore took it upon herself to begin to criticize her brother because of the woman he had chosen to marry.

Numbers 12:1-15
1 Then Miriam and Aaron spoke against Moses because of the
Ethiopian woman whom he had married; for he had married an
Ethiopian woman.
2 So they said, "has the Lord indeed spoken only through Moses?
Has He not spoken through us also?" And the Lord heard it.
9 So the anger of the Lord was aroused against them, and he
departed.
10 And when the cloud departed from above the tabernacle,
suddenly Miriam became leprous, as white as snow. Then Aaron
turned toward Miriam, and there she was, a leper.
15 So Miriam was shut out of the camp seven days, and the people
did not journey till Miriam was brought in again.

God's argument was that the relationship Moses had with Him was not ordinary and He asked them "Why then were you not afraid to speak against **My** servant Moses?"

DON'T FAIL TO MAKE THE TRANSITION

What was Aaron's and Miriam's problem? It was familiarity. They knew Moses as their brother and had not made the transition to respect him as their leader.

Women who have had a hard time respecting those in authority and especially male authority figures in their lives, can transfer those same emotions into their relationship with their pastors.

Jesus Himself experienced disrespect when He went to His hometown in Galilee. The Scripture records that when He went to his hometown where He had grown up, the people only saw Him as the son of Joseph and Mary. They referred to His brothers and sisters who still lived there. And as a result of their refusal to respect Him, He could not do any great miracles there. He was restrained in His ability and could only heal a few people with minor illnesses.

The extent to which you will be able to receive from your pastor will depend on the extent to which you will honor and respect him.

The Woman and Her Pastor

CHAPTER 6

BUILDING BLOCK #4
HONOR YOUR PASTOR

1 Tim. 5:17 - 19 says: "Let the elders that rule well be counted worthy of double honor..." The context here is in the realm of finances. We are expected to deduce from this that the pastor must be well looked after. He must not look poor. He must not look worse than any other executive in the city. If our executives in the secular world can drive nice cars, live in beautiful houses, and wear well tailored suits of good quality, our pastors should be considered worthy of double honor.

Some of us grew up in a society where we were taught that the pastor should be poor in order to identify with the people. It is hard for us to understand that if we keep our pastor poor, we too will remain poor because the anointing flows from the head down. Women made up a great part of the ministry of Jesus. They gave of their substance to him. Nothing was too expensive. It could be a box of alabaster ointment, or ointment of spikenard. Women in the church today must learn how to bless their pastor. You do not need to have an occasion to give him a love offering. Just do it.

To honor also means to appreciate. The problem we have in churches today is that our churches are willing to appreciate everybody _ the visiting speaker or the television evangelist, but they do not appreciate their own pastor.

To honor also means to admire. You can admire without lusting. Find something that you can admire in your pastor such as his commitment to the Word or to prayer or to his family. Find something to admire about him while understanding that no one man can have everything that you are seeking to find in a pastor.

I remember that, apart from his good looks, the other thing that attracted me to my husband was his preaching. Over the years I have found out that my husband can do some things really well but he was not as knowledgeable about other things such as cooking. Recently, he discovered that he does enjoy cooking his favorite meals on occasion.

Nevertheless, I have learned to major in and magnify those things which I love about him. He is a loving husband who does whatever he must to make me laugh when I'm sad. He loves our children and works hard to provide for them and to leave an inheritance for them as the Word admonishes in Proverbs 13:22. He prides himself on being my personal handyman able to fix anything that needs repairing around the home.

I know that many women would be glad to trade husbands with me and many women may be glad to trade husbands with you too. While you are complaining that your husband neglects you when he goes fishing, some other woman is crying because her husband has been neglecting her over another woman. There will always be faults that we can find if we look for them but there are also good qualities

which we can find if we look diligently for them.

I have always remembered the anecdote I heard once about a

wicked man who died and no one could find anything good to say

about him. But one man who always practiced finding the good in

others, when asked to give his opinion of the dead man, simply said,

"He had nice eyes."

In the same manner, find what is admirable in your pastor and

keep it before you.

To honor also means to defer to another person. It also means

to yield. When you come to a crossroad and your pastor makes a

decision that you do not agree with, you are supposed to defer to him

or yield to him. When you are in traffic and you come to a yield sign,

do you insist on pressing ahead? You don't because you know great

injury can be caused to you and the other driver if you do so. Many

pastors and members of congregations have been mortally injured

because the membership did not understand headship. They were never taught that in the long run the right to make the final decision, right or wrong, belongs to their pastor. Defer to your pastor.

Esteem your pastor. Paul admonishes us in 1 Thess. 5:12-13 "to respect those who labor among you and are over you in the Lord and admonish you, and to esteem them very highly in love because of their work (RSV).

To esteem is to value and to have great regard for. If you consider your pastor to be valuable to you, it will affect the way you treat him. You will not want to lose him because you place a great price on him. But notice that according to the apostle Paul, the estimation of your pastor is not dependent upon his personality, but upon the work that he is doing. Your pastor's personality and yours may clash, but your decision to honor him is not to be dependent on personality but on performance. Is he feeding the flock? Are lives being changed? Is he functioning in the calling of the Lord? Then, your responsibility is to honor him.

The Woman and Her Pastor

CHAPTER 7

BUILDING BLOCK #5
DEFEND YOUR PASTOR

Psalms 127: 4-5
4 Children born to a young man are like sharp arrows to defend him.
5 Happy is the man who has his quiver full of them. That man shall
have the help he needs when arguing with his enemies.
TLB

King David compared children to arrows in the hand of a warrior. By comparison, your pastor is like your father and the members of the church are his children. The purpose of children is to defend their fathers from his enemies. When they were young, the father defended them, but when they become grown up, they are to come to the defense of their father.

ARROWS... NOT BOOMERANGS

Your pastor should never have to defend himself in the public.

His children, the members of his church, who sit under his ministry,

should defend him when people in the community want to malign him.

It is very rare that you hear anyone, ill-speak his father to the general

public. We have heard of fights that broke out between children

because one child claimed that his daddy was stronger, taller, and

better than the other child's daddy. Some of us have had natural

fathers that neglected us or mistreated us and yet we hold it secret.

We do not get on national TV and tell about the misdeeds of our

fathers.

Sadly in the church, this is not so. The children join with their

father's enemies in destroying his reputation and in shredding his

public image.

Church members sometimes have no compunction about

discussing their pastor's faults, real or imagined with other members

as well as non-members and worse still, sinners. Instead of being

arrows directed at those who seek to harm their pastors, they turn on their pastors themselves. So many pastors are discovering that what they have in their quiver are not arrows but boomerangs.

A TIME TO DEFEND

When should you defend your pastor? – at all times. You may say he needs no defense. Neither does the gospel and yet Paul said that he was set for the defense of the gospel. (Phil 1:16)

You are to believe the best of your pastor until he proves otherwise and this proof must not be based on the testimony of just one or two individuals. Secondly if your pastor is proven to be guilty of an offense, you should still stand with him and defend him once he is repentant. Do not cast him out to the dogs. Do not leave him wounded in the battlefield for his enemies to capture and torment him. Defend your pastor.

"But", you may ask, "Why should I put my hand in the fire for my pastor when he is just a man like I am?" That is exactly the point! HE IS A MAN and prone to the failures of men. And what is Jesus doing for you with all your imperfections and failings? He is acting as your advocate, your defense lawyer before the Righteous Judge of all the earth. Therefore if Jesus who knew no sin can come to your defense before His Righteous and Just Father, why can't you who have your own struggles and imperfections come to your pastor's defense before people who are also imperfect and unrighteous?

Paul was grieved when at his first defense, no one stood with him.

2 Timothy 4:16
16 At my first trial no one acted in my defense [as my advocate] or took my part or [even] stood with me, but all forsook me. May it not be charged against them!
AMP

Can you imagine that? The mighty apostle Paul, from whose body handkerchiefs would be sent out to those who were sick, and they would be healed, did not find one Christian in the whole city of Rome or its environs to stand with him in his hour of accusation. How sad! Yet this is played out again and again in our churches. Pastors come under attack. Satan, the accuser, seeks to find an accusation against the man of God and the man of God reaches behind his back to find an arrow, only to discover that his quiver is empty or his arrows are dull and ineffective, or much worse, his arrows have turned into knives which his enemies have stuck in his back.

SONS AND HIRELINGS

If we could take a survey of how many good men and women have been destroyed, or who have aborted their ministries because those whom they thought were sons turned out to be hirelings, it would surprise you. But it is such a joy when you have sons who come to your defense. I remember once that someone my husband was affiliated with was speaking badly about him to one of our members not knowing that the individual was actually one of our musicians. This son not only came to our defense but alerted us of what this person was wrongfully accusing us.

Over the years of ministering, we have been blessed to have raised many sons and daughters. They have been misunderstood by others. They have been accused of being messenger boys of the pastor, but it did not deter them from functioning as true sons and daughters.

I read a book some time ago entitled "Inside the Magic Kingdom" by Tom Connellan. In it he elaborated on what has contributed to the success of Disneyworld. He talks about "the culture" that each employee or "cast member" (as they prefer to call their employees) absorbs. One aspect of their culture, is that it is the responsibility of everyone to be eyes and ears for the "Kingdom". "Customers are best heard through many ears". If it's true for the Magic Kingdom, is it not true for the Kingdom of God? Will not our churches be better off if each member becomes ears and eyes for his pastor, so that guests return to us again and again as they do to Disneyworld?

Defend your pastor and be a true son. Become his eyes and ears and so increase his effectiveness in the Kingdom.

The Woman and Her Pastor

The Woman and Her Pastor

CHAPTER 8

BUILDING BLOCK #6
SERVE YOUR PASTOR,
HIS WIFE AND HIS CHILDREN

If you want to develop a positive relationship with your pastor,

learn to serve him, his wife and his children.

The apostles in the early church soon realized that if they tried

to do everything by themselves, they would become worn out. So they

appointed in the church seven deacons, men who were full of faith, of

good report and full of the Holy Ghost. These men's job was not to

preach but to help the apostles handle the administrative aspects of

the church such as waiting on, or serving tables.

Phoebe was called a servant of the church (Romans 16: 1 - 3). Paul commended her to the church at Rome on this basis. When you are a servant of the church, you are in fact a servant of the pastor. You need to learn to serve the men and women of God. Many times, people in the church and outside of the church are draining them by constantly pulling on them. People come for prayer, and for counsel. They are umpiring strife within the church and within marriages.

Jesus had women who ministered to or served him. Joshua, before he was called to lead Israel into the Promised Land was known as the servant of Moses. Elisha was known only as the person who poured water on the hands of Elijah.

> **2 Kings 3:11**
> *Here is Elisha the son of Shaphat, which poured water on the hands of Elijah.*
> *KJV*

Yet when the time came for Elijah to be caught up to heaven, it was Elisha who received the double portion of the anointing that was on Elijah.

Serving your pastor and his family is looked upon by God as a sign that there is greatness in you. In fact the Lord promises a reward for receiving them and ministering to them.

Matt 10:40-42
41 He who receives a prophet because he is a prophet shall receive a prophet's reward, and he who receives a righteous man because he is a righteous man shall receive a righteous man's reward.
RSV

When you serve your pastor, you refresh him. You help to prevent him from feeling burnt out and unappreciated.

HELP A SISTER OUT

Learn to help his wife too. If she does not have paid help, offer to do the laundry sometimes or some ironing or just give her a day's cleaning. Offer to take care of the children for a while so that she can have a day to herself. A happy, appreciated pastor's wife leads to a happy pastor and a happy pastor will serve his people with joy.

I have been blessed during my years in ministry with many people who have come into my life just to be a help to me. There have been times when I felt as though I was at the end of my rope. I could not take any more and the Lord just sent someone into my life. This person just volunteered her time or service whether it was in office work, or at the home or helping with my children. These acts of service inevitably endeared that person to me. Primarily because I am an "acts of service" kind of person. I show love by acts of service and I interpret being loved by acts of service. If you have been trying to get close to your pastor's wife, this might be one of the ways that you can do so.

DON'T FORGET THE KIDS

What can we say about his children? Many times pastors' children grow up with a feeling of ambivalence towards the church or develop an outright rebellious attitude towards it and all that it represents. Sometimes this is the fault of their parents who neglected them in the interest of "the work of the Lord" – not realizing that their first duty is towards their family and not towards the Lord's bride. However in other instances, people in the church put so much pressure on pastors' children that the children become resentful.

Pastors' children are just like every other child in the church. They need to be saved, filled with the Holy Spirit and grow in grace and in the knowledge of Jesus Christ. They need to develop Christian maturity just like you and your children do. Church members somehow get the impression that pastor's children are supposed to have some magical or spiritual power that will make them exempt from the normal faults and failings of other children and impress upon these children the need to be "an example". They must walk right, talk right, dress right and always, always behave right because they are the pastor's children. Other children may or may not do certain things but the eyes of everyone are upon the pastor's children and so it is more likely that they will be seen before any other child who commits any wrong doing.

My husband and I raised four sons and one daughter while pastoring our church. Now that some of them are grown, they are more ready to share some of the feelings they had towards church members while they were young. I think that people think that children will not remember the things that were done to them or said to them. But they do. The pastor's children will remember you. How will they remember you? Will they remember you as someone who was always positive towards them or someone who was always ready to put them down and criticize them?

I remember one of my boys describing a very active sister in the church as mean. Even today, he does not have very happy memories about that sister. Just recently, I was astonished by the level of animosity that one of my children felt towards someone whom he had known for many years. Of course, I lectured him on the need to walk in forgiveness, but at the same time, I had to apologize to him for my insensitivity to his reality all those years.

Am I saying that pastors should not discipline their children? Of course not! One of the requirements for becoming a bishop is that he must rule his household well. (1Timothy 3:4) But how many of you have children who do most of what you say but there is one who will go in a different direction in spite of all you do and say? It happens in the house of the pastor as well and he is not necessarily responsible for the decisions that any of his children may take at some point in their lives.

TAKE THE TIME TO LOVE

How can you help? Serve the pastor's children. Invite them over to your house for a barbecue or take the smaller ones to their favorite eating place. Let them remember the church by the people who gave them a good time and not by those who they perceived to be constantly nagging them and finding fault with them. What they don't understand is that they will find all kinds of people in the world and that the church is just a sampling of the kinds of personalities that exist in the world. However because this is their only world_ the place where most of their life is experienced, they tend to form the opinion that "church people" are in some way less desirable than people "on the outside". And this is not just true of the pastor's kids but of most children who are raised in church and who to a large extent are sheltered from the real world.

Too many pastors' children have been traumatized in their parents' church. Some of them ended up walking away from the church never to return. It is a sad story that has been repeated more times than you want to know. The question is would some of these children have stayed if more people in the church had taken the time to just love them without labeling them? My next question is, will you be that person for your pastor's children?

CHAPTER 9

BUILDING BLOCK #7
CONSERVE YOUR PASTOR'S
TIME AND ENERGY

Some people thrive on getting other people's attention. Parents, pastors and doctors are prime targets for those in this category. However, while a doctor can demand a fee from you for every time you required his services, a pastor is expected to be on call twenty-four hours a day, seven days a week, fifty-two weeks a year at no extra charge. Because of this, pastors are very often the objects of abuse.

The apostle Paul, in Philippians 4:2 implored Euodia and Synteche to "agree and work in harmony in the Lord." (Amplified). When supposedly mature people in the Lord refuse to respond to each other biblically, it drains the pastor's energy and time. The Scripture outlines the method for dealing with offenses. First you talk to the person alone, then you take a witness, finally, if the person will still not hear, you take him to the church (leadership).

Matt 18:15-17

15 "If your brother sins against you, go and show him his fault, just between the two of you. If he listens to you, you have won your brother over.
16 But if he will not listen, take one or two others along, so that 'every matter may be established by the testimony of two or three witnesses.'
17 If he refuses to listen to them, tell it to the church; and if he refuses to listen even to the church, treat him as you would a pagan or a tax collector.
NIV

Moreover if you are not the offended one but you feel you might have offended somebody, the Scripture also gives you the formula for dealing with such circumstances.

The Living Bible puts it this way.

Matt 5:23-24

23 "So if you are standing before the altar in the Temple, offering a sacrifice to God, and suddenly remember that a friend has something against you,
24 leave your sacrifice there beside the altar and go and apologize and be reconciled to him, and then come and offer your sacrifice to God.
TLB

TIME VALUED... TIME WASTED

The pastor's time should not be wasted in having to settle frivolous arguments between mature Christians who should know better. The pastor is not a fireman. Do not be a fire setter but be a fire wetter_ extinguish them.

Christian people must grow up. It is not necessary to call the pastor for every toothache, headache and backache. There should be able individuals in the church who can handle minor problems. There should be able ministers or deacons in the church who can handle minor family crises.

Moses' father-in-law, Jethro, warned Moses about wearing himself and the people out by attempting to handle every case. He urged Moses to choose other men from the congregation of Israel to handle the people's needs and to handle only the hard cases himself.

Ex 18:17-23

17 Moses' father in law replied, "What you are doing is not good.
18 You and these people who come to you will only wear yourselves out. The work is too heavy for you; you cannot handle it alone.
19 Listen now to me and I will give you some advice, and may God be with you. You must be the people's representative before God and bring their disputes to him.
20 Teach them the decrees and laws, and show them the way to live and the duties they are to perform.
21 But select capable men from all the people, men who fear God, trustworthy men who hate dishonest gain and appoint them as officials over thousands, hundreds, fifties and tens.
22 Have them serve as judges for the people at all times, but have them bring every difficult case to you; the simple cases they can decide themselves. That will make your load lighter, because they will share it with you.
23 If you do this and God so commands, you will be able to stand the strain, and all these people will go home satisfied."
NIV

But how many of you get offended when the pastor does not personally visit or call you when you are sick? And those of you who visit the sick and home-bound members, do you let them know that you are representing the pastor? Or do you try to make it appear that he has forgotten them but you have not?

HOLD ON, LET ME CALL MY PASTOR

How many people are guilty of using the pastor as a telephone directory or Bible Concordance? Some pastors have taken the step of having an unlisted telephone number. Although everyone may not be in agreement with this, we have to wonder what experiences may have contributed to a pastor taking such a step. People call at the most inopportune times and for the strangest reasons. One person called our home at 2:00 a.m. to ask my husband where a certain verse could be found in the Bible. Others have awakened us on holidays and weekends because they wanted to pray with us. Actions such as these may be well-meaning but they are certainly thoughtless and unwise. Church members need to understand that their pastors have a life too.

VALUING HIS TIME

Do you know that in most churches people show up late for counseling appointments, wedding rehearsals and weddings? Do you know that if pastors were to charge people by the hour, they would overcome their habitual lateness? But pastors are taken for granted. They are expected to wait until people show up and if the pastor does not, church members are offended. As a matter of fact you should not just walk in on your pastor unannounced. You ought to treat him with as much respect as you show to any professional person and make an appointment to see him except if it is an emergency.

Do not expect your pastor to attend every meeting that there is at the church. Even though the pastor should be kept abreast of what is happening in every department of the church, it is not necessary for him to attend every men's meeting, women's meeting and youth meeting.

We need to conserve our pastor's time and energy. In so doing he will live longer to be a blessing to us.

THE EARLY CHURCH

The early church had to make a decision to do this for the apostles. In the book of Acts we are told that murmuring and complaining arose because the Grecians felt that their widows were being neglected. Peter had to take leadership and tell the church that they needed to assign men full of the Holy Ghost to take care of this business and so free the apostles to give their attention to prayer and the Word. So when you volunteer, you are actually conserving your pastor's time and energy and allowing him to be more effective at what God has called him to do. Do it graciously and with a willing heart because God has a reward for you equivalent to the reward He has for the man of God just because you might have given him a cup of cold water.

The Woman and Her Pastor

CHAPTER 10

BUILDING BLOCK #8
PROTECT YOUR PASTOR'S REPUTATION

No one can destroy a person's character because that is what he is even if no one knows anything about him. But someone can destroy a person's reputation because that is what he is in the eyes of people.

Many men of God have been unable to continue their work for God or are no longer able to be effective in the ministry because they have lost their reputation or their reputation has been destroyed by lies, slander, innuendoes, gossip and other destructive uses of the tongue.

We do not need to be reminded of the scandals that have rocked the Church in the past, however I do want to remind women that you have a vital role to play in protecting your pastor's reputation. Most pastors are good men with a fatherly heart. However, we must always remember that all male pastors are men. By this I mean, that they too are subject to infirmities and temptations of the flesh. In their role as counselor, it is quite possible for the women they counsel to transfer very strong emotions to their pastor. It is a known fact that in the counseling experience, the counselee can begin to believe that the relationship with her counselor is more than a platonic one. Women have been known to fall in love with their doctors, counselors, and pastors. This is a difficult situation but it becomes even worse when these professional people reciprocate and break up their marriages and their families by giving in to an illicit relationship.

WISE WOMEN PROTECT

Women in the church need to help their pastor by discouraging visits to their homes when no one else is present, by dressing appropriately in his presence and by not giving people an occasion to doubt his integrity.

If you are a single woman you must practice wisdom in how you approach your pastor for help. Do not expect the pastor to run all kinds of errands for you, especially any that will necessitate his coming into your apartment. Do not become a regular fixture in his vehicle. Do not be a source of temptation to him by sitting in the passenger's seat in short skirts and short pants. Do not entertain him alone at your home for any reason. Such actions can lead to questions in people's minds.

It is sad that even though a man of God can innocently proffer help to the female members of their congregations, he can be deceived and even fall into sin when he had no intention or thought of doing so. As women of God, we need to be wise and to protect our pastor's reputation. The Word of the Lord clearly tells us that we are to "adorn the doctrine of God Our Savior in all things" (Titus 2:10) and that we must make sure that our good is not spoken evil of". (Romans

14:6)

If you get to the place where you feel that your pastor needs

you in the ministry more than he needs his wife or that you are such

an important prayer warrior that the pastor has to be with you in

prayer on a regular basis privately, you are treading on dangerous

ground. It is only a matter of time before Satan will set a trap for you

and before you know it your pastor's reputation will have been

destroyed through the open door which you have created. Protect

your pastor's reputation.

DISENGAGE FROM THE NEGATIVE

Another way you can protect your pastor's reputation is by

refusing to engage in any conversation in which others are discussing

him in a negative way. If something comes to your attention that you

feel can be damaging to your pastor's reputation, you should make him

aware of it instead of discussing it with others. Set an appointment

with your pastor. Assure your pastor of your love for him. Let him know what you have heard. Let him know that you believe in him and that you are sharing what you have heard so that he can take whatever steps he needs to take in order to avert a crisis. Once you have done this continue to pray for your pastor.

I should add that this does not mean that you bother your pastor about everything you hear about him. This does not mean that you become a tattler. There are times I hear things that people have said concerning my husband. I deal with it. I don't disturb him about every report that I have heard. I share only those things that I feel need his personal input in order to be resolved or that he ought to be aware of in order to know how to deal wisely with a particular individual. As I said earlier, you can measure those things that should be shared by asking yourself whether it is something that can damage his reputation if steps are not taken to resolve the issue.

Don't be alarmed if your pastor does not do anything with what you have shared with him. There are times when men and women of God will allow gossip to run its course. There are times when to dignify something with a response will only give it more power. Men and women of God have learned that many times it is necessary to emulate the pattern of Jesus as recorded in 1 Peter 2.

1 Peter 2:23

23 who, when He was reviled, did not revile in return; when He suffered, He did not threaten, but committed Himself to Him who judges righteously;
NKJV

LOVE COVERS

The failure to respond, or retaliate is not an admission of guilt. However if your pastor has been behaving inappropriately and after you have shared with him, he makes no attempt to seek to correct his actions, then you may need to confide in another pastor whom your pastor considers as a mentor.

Above all remember that "love covers a multitude of sins" and that we should under no circumstances take our pastor's failings or sins out before the courtroom of the world.

Let's look at how it is read in 1 Corinthians 6:1-4:

1 Cor 6:1-4

6:1 How is it that when you have something against another Christian, you "go to law" and ask a heathen court to decide the matter instead of taking it to other Christians to decide which of you is right?
2 Don't you know that someday we Christians are going to judge and govern the world? So why can't you decide even these little things among yourselves?
3 Don't you realize that we Christians will judge and reward the very angels in heaven? So you should be able to decide your problems down here on earth easily enough.
TLB

Even though the exact context of this is concerning taking brothers to court, I believe that the spirit of the Word also infers that we should not take the affairs of our church into the open forum of the "pavilion of men's tongues". (Psa. 31:20)

Protect your pastor's reputation because nothing can happen to him that will not affect you.

The Woman and Her Pastor

CHAPTER 11

BUILDING BLOCK #9
DO NOT COMPETE WITH
YOUR PASTOR

Avoid competing with your pastor, it is the spirit of Absalom.

More churches have been destroyed by this spirit than people know.

It is because the spirit of Absalom is a very deceitful and devious spirit.

People who have this spirit are usually very "lovable" and "loving"

people. They appear to be very concerned about the well-being of the

church and its members. People who have an Absalom spirit do not

make their move until they have become entrenched in the hearts of

the people and the pastor will appear to be ungrateful and

unreasonable to remove them from whatever position they hold in the church. David's son, Absalom, won the hearts of the people of Israel away from his father.

2 Sam 15:1-6

1 In the course of time, Absalom provided himself with a chariot and horses and with fifty men to run ahead of him.
2 He would get up early and stand by the side of the road leading to the city gate. Whenever anyone came with a complaint to be placed before the king for a decision, Absalom would call out to him, "What town are you from?" He would answer, "Your servant is from one of the tribes of Israel."
3 Then Absalom would say to him, "Look, your claims are valid and proper, but there is no representative of the king to hear you."
4 And Absalom would add, "If only I were appointed judge in the land! Then everyone who has a complaint or case could come to me and I would see that he gets justice."
5 Also, whenever anyone approached him to bow down before him, Absalom would reach out his hand, take hold of him and kiss him.
6 Absalom behaved in this way toward all the Israelites who came to the king asking for justice, and so he stole the hearts of the men of Israel.
NIV

Absalom then waited four years before plotting the overthrow of his father.

SENSITIVE YET SUBMISSIVE

Sometimes as women, we feel that we are so sensitive to the Spirit of God. We may have a prophetic anointing upon our lives or a healing anointing. Our pastor, may not have either of these gifts of the Spirit operating in his life. However, we are not here to compete with him. God did not set us in the church to be a competitor. We must learn how to function in a submissive spirit, especially if we have a man of God who is willing to allow us to function in our calling. For heaven's sake, let's not use our gift to compete with him. Don't try to belittle your pastor. If you believe you have a word from the Lord, run it by your pastor before releasing it to the congregation. You are not there to make yourself look good at his expense. You are not there to make the rest of the congregation lose respect for him because you come across as the one who has all the gifts while your pastor is a sad comparison. Your gifts are meant to edify not destroy. I remember a woman at our church who had the gift of the word of knowledge operating in her life especially for the healing of bodily ailments. Yet she had such a humble, submissive spirit that she would always approach my husband and tell him what she perceived. She did not

want the microphone. She would have been quite content to allow the

pastor to describe the physical conditions. My husband would give her

the microphone to say what she saw. After that she left it up to him to

pray with the people who identified themselves. At that time my

husband did not flow in that gifting. Now he flows in the Word of

knowledge to a greater degree than this dear woman of God. But she

was never his competitor.

WHEN JEALOUSY MANIFESTS

Jealousy also manifests itself in a competitive spirit. Aaron and

Miriam, Moses' biological brother and sister were guilty of this.

Numbers 12:1-2

12:1 Miriam and Aaron began to talk against Moses because of his
Cushite wife, for he had married a Cushite. 2 "Has the LORD spoken
only through Moses?" they asked. "Hasn't he also spoken through
us?" And the LORD heard this.
NIV

If you know the rest of the story, you know what happened

after the Lord heard. He struck Miriam with leprosy and the whole nation was kept back for seven days until the Lord healed Miriam and restored her. Do not become jealous of your pastor. The Lord may bless him with a new house or a new car. Do not allow this to stir up resentment and jealousy in your heart so that you begin to speak against him. He is the Lord's servant and it is the prerogative of the Lord to bless him as He sees fit. Do not be critical of him because of his personal preferences as were Miriam and Aaron concerning Moses' choice of a wife. Do not become jealous of the revelations that the Lord gives to him and the authority that he wields as a servant of the Lord.

DANGEROUS GROUND

A competitive spirit leads to a rebellious spirit as in the case of Korah.

Num 16:1-3

1 Korah son of Izhar, the son of Kohath, the son of Levi, and certain Reubenites--Dathan and Abiram, sons of Eliab, and On son of Peleth--became insolent
2 and rose up against Moses. With them were 250 Israelite men, well-known community leaders who had been appointed members of the council.
3 They came as a group to oppose Moses and Aaron and said to

99

them, "You have gone too far! The whole community is holy, every one of them, and the LORD is with them. Why then do you set yourselves above the LORD's assembly?"
NIV

They accused Moses and Aaron as setting themselves above the Lord's assembly and they stirred up a rebellion in the camp. They wanted to compete with Moses. What was the end of that? God sent an earthquake and swallowed the whole group. Not only were they destroyed, but their wives and children as well.

When you give in to a spirit of competition, you endanger the destiny of your entire family because competitiveness is a yoke-fellow of jealousy and rebellion. Rebellion is a very dangerous spirit. That is why God deals so decisively with those who allow themselves to be ruled by such a spirit. It is compared to the sin of witchcraft.

Rebellion in a church can open the door to sickness and even the death of your pastor. Therefore, when God sees the meekness of his servant and he bows his knee to the Lord to complain about the injustice of church members, the sickness or death which may have come upon him, returns to those who were the perpetrators. Do not try to compete with your pastor, it is the spirit of Absalom.

The Woman and Her Pastor

CHAPTER 12

BUILDING BLOCK #10
DO NOT TRY TO CONTROL
YOUR PASTOR

Some women never compete with their pastor but they try to

control him. A controlling woman is a Jezebel. Contrary to what was

taught in the old school, a Jezebel is not someone who wears a lot of

make-up. You can wear make-up from your eyebrows to your chin and

wear rings and even bells on your toes, yet be free from a Jezebel spirit.

A Jezebel spirit is a spirit of control. Jezebel controlled her husband,

and by extension she controlled the kingdom of Israel.

She usurped her husband's authority and made decisions and decreed things about which he knew nothing and about which he was not consulted. She denigrated her husband to a weak and feeble position and eroded his authority and his headship as her husband and as king. Yet she did it under the guise of doing it for him.

NOT SO GOOD INTENTIONS

Likewise, in the church, seemingly well-intentioned women can seek to control the man of God. They seek to do so through gifts given with an ulterior motive and through apparent acts of service. They seek to infiltrate positions of authority from which they attempt to manipulate the pastor and decide the direction of the ministry.

You may have ideas and suggestions, you may even be able to offer advice to the pastor in an area of expertise in which he may be unfamiliar, but that does not give you the right to control him. The final decision is still the pastor's.

<u>YOUR RESPONSIBILTY IS TO FLOW</u>

You may not agree with his decision. However once the decision is made, your responsibility is to flow with it and to seek to bring the vision of the pastor to come to pass.

Let us say that you serve on the office staff of the church. You may be computer literate and your pastor is not. Or you may have a wonderful grasp of accounting principles and your pastor does not. If you are reprimanded for late-coming or absenteeism and you threaten to resign, knowing that you will put the ministry at a serious disadvantage if you do so, you are displaying a Jezebel attitude. If you use your knowledge and the pastor's lack of knowledge concerning these things to hijack the ministry or hold the pastor hostage, you are operating with a spirit of control.

You may be the only decent organist at your church and a blessing in the praise and worship but your pastor may make some change in the order of the service. If, because he has done so, you resign from the music department, you may be operating by a spirit of control.

SPIRIT OF CONTROL

Controlling individuals can actually become physically sick when they cannot have their own way or when responsibilities are taken away from them and given to another. They oppose any change which will lessen their ability to exercise control over the ministry.

They may use tears, argument, sympathy, withholding of time, talent or tithes and other controlling behavior. They may try to put up a front of humility but invariably, they use the pronouns "I" and "me" much more than "we and "us".

If they are not discerned and neutralized, they can sabotage the entire ministry and destroy the pastor. In the many years that my husband and I have had the opportunity to pastor, we have seen many things take place in our ministry as well as in the ministries of other pastors.

We have seen churches split, members scattered and years of work destroyed because of a spirit of control operating in someone who either knowingly or unknowingly allowed the devil to use them in this way.

This is the crux of the matter. Even though you may be doing a good thing, you may be doing it in the wrong place. I recently read Dr. Mac Hammond's _Principles of Leadership_ in which he pointed out that if your vision or passion does not fall in line with the vision of the pastor over that local body, if you seek to influence people to finance or support your vision without the approval of the pastor, you are being divisive. In fact, Dr. Hammond goes on to say that it is better that you find another church where your vision lines up with the pastor of that local body, than for you to stay where you are, initiating plans that are not on your pastor's schedule or program.

I was set free from a lot of guilt when I understood that while we are all called to ministry, some of us have been given greater responsibility or vision in certain areas. Therefore some churches reflect the passion of their pastor for foreign missions, or prayer, or evangelism. These are all good and necessary and should be included in every church but the emphasis may vary from church to church. Every church that Jesus addressed in Revelation, was commended for something that they were passionate about. Every church that the

Apostle Paul wrote to, had its particular flavor. Every church is not for everyone. That is why you must ask God to place you in a local body that is a good fit for you. And above all, if you want to foster a good relationship with your pastor, do not try to control him, it is indicative of a Jezebel spirit.

CONCLUSION

"I trust that this book has been a blessing to you and that once you have identified yourself, you will allow the Holy Spirit to do a work of grace in your heart to make you into a true blessing to your pastor. Women have a vital role to play in the church. The Lord has need of us. Therefore we must not allow ourselves to be manipulated by the devil and used by him to stir up trouble or division in the church. Rather let us be remembered as the Abigail, the Ruth, the Dorcas, the Priscilla, the Anna, the woman with the alabaster box, and so many others who made an impact in biblical history."

Marcia

About the Author

Pastor Marcia Judith Estrada was born on the island of Trinidad in the Republic of Trinidad and Tobago. She was born again at the age of eight and has served the Lord faithfully since then.

She and her husband, Apostle Ashley Estrada, have been pastors for over 35 years. They are the founding pastors of Kingdom Life International Christian Center in St. Thomas Virgin Islands and Poinciana, Florida.

Pastor Marcia is the mother of five children and four grand-children. She holds a Diploma from the West Indies School of Theology in Trinidad, a Bachelor's Degree in Psychology from the University of the Virgin Islands, St. Thomas and a Masters' Degree in Biblical Counseling from Trinity Seminary. She has ministered in several women's conferences and in leadership conferences and is known for having a powerful anointed word to the Body of Christ in general, and to women in the Body of Christ in particular.

35744599R00064

Made in the USA
San Bernardino, CA
03 July 2016